HOW DEEP IS LOVE

ALAN KEMP

How Deep Is Love
is available on Lulu.com
Amazon, and Barnes & Noble

Contact Information:

FB address:
https://www.facebook.com/alan.kemp.568

Email
kempy123@live.co.uk

Contact Information for Publisher,
Wildfire Publications:
poetrystarz@hotmail.com

DEDICATION

By Alan Kemp

There are many people who deserve my thanks, gratitude and respect for the immeasurable support and love they have shown toward me in the creation of this little book. Not least to Allison and the kids and those that have prayerfully been behind me from before I was even saved and have continued to intercede on my behalf.

Then there's the faithfulness and wonder of God shown to me through Susan Joyner-Stumpf in her active encouragement and selfless support by way of actually enabling my writing to reach these pages.

Ultimately I give God all the praise, honor and glory believing that He will use these poems to connect with those in need.

TABLE OF CONTENTS

FOREWORD

Looking at Alan and I during our first 20 years together, we really had very little in common except our 3 beautiful children. Alan wanted money and a good lifestyle; I wanted a family life and to spend quality time with my husband, not for him to work all the hours under the sun, rarely seeing his children awake.

Thankfully, God has a master plan, and, after 20 years of prayer for Alan, I was with him when he gave his life to God, and our New life began. Alan's priorities changed to focus on God's will, and he has been given a gift of sharing the impact God has had in our lives through verse.

The journey has not always been easy, as the devil never takes a day off, and has thrown problem after problem our way, but God has never left us to cope alone. In fact, when we are walking closely with God, that is often when we come under greatest attack. I believe through these poems you will see hope become reality, and tears turn to joy, and peace reign.

These poems have been written to reach the lost, those hurting and those who feel hopeless, while encouraging the Christian in their personal walk with God. These poems are for the ordinary person like me, who has made the decision to work for the man with the master plan.

Never give up, God is in control.

Allison

PREFACE

<u>GOD DOESN'T MAKE JUNK</u>

My only real memory of "parents" is of them fighting, a mother being abused, a father drinking, drunk, possessed by something ugly. I can't relate to a feeling of being loved or part of a "family." Happiness and pain were beaten out of me one way or another along the way. My Dad was a businessman with money and plenty of it; he sure knew how to spend it on himself and put on a show. A big house but no "home" and fast cars but no "family" road trips. At primary school, I felt like I didn't belong, as I could roam the streets all day and no one seemed to miss me!

By the time I was at grammar school, the parental warfare had peaked and my father appeared more and more comforted by money and alcohol. They were separated officially now (whatever that means) and as a young boy whilst you don't understand the why (do you ever), you fully realize the what!

I became steadily more cold and bitter, rebelling against authority in very subtle ways, as I always knew best and through time, right into married life, I became more selfish and controlling. I wasn't nice to live with; was I becoming just like my Dad? I have a brother and sister but we all lived separate lives. By the time I hit 16, I had no emotional connection with any one and made choices to live life in the fast lane. I was drinking and clubbing 5 nights a week, living it up, but not content. Any rush from what I abused my body with didn't last and didn't repair low self-esteem or soften my heart that's for sure.

By now my mind or what was left of it, was set even more on doing things my way and my heart was empty. I still have memories of Sundays as the day when Dad would arrive, at some point, held back sometimes, by the obligatory restraining order! The majority of the past is locked away, never to be remembered, but I distinctly recall one particular Sunday afternoon my Dad was driving us to Nan's for dinner, although he was so drunk he thought he was racing a chariot and was gesturing as if cracking a whip to make us go faster. We did: a lot faster, easily over 100m.p.h, and then skidding and spinning, we ended up wrapping around a sign post and miraculously, no one was hurt. At least not physically. Similar Journeys happened on many, many Sundays with miraculously no other accidents. Now that's the hand of God at work. I also remember being missed by inches by a drunk driver outside my house, more irony or more of God. Anyway, I did it, I made it to the University as far away from home as I could get. Here, on day one, I met Allison, a girl far away from her Northern Ireland home, now in my native England, and one way or another, we hit it off. I don't know how; we argued at the start over religion, the troubles in Northern Ireland and whether God was real. Of course I was right, Religion was dangerous, Northern Ireland was a lost cause and God couldn't possibly be real.

That was 1988. I was 18, fast forward a little, and by 1991, we had been together for 3 years and I moved to Northern Ireland to settle down. By 1993, we were married. Marriage, now that's some subject, don't you think? What good had I ever seen of marriage, it was hardly a strong advert for "holy matrimony" don't you think?

The marriage thing wasn't exactly straight forward. Firstly, I wasn't very keen on that ceremonial stuff, just to prove my love. I may well have lost the ability to express emotion, but inside, I was in love and somehow Allison got that and could see past my cold exterior.

As time went on, we had three amazing children, Poppy, Amber and Peter, who, looking back, are only here by the grace of God and the power of prayer from so many close to Allison. Soon after Peter was born, he was very ill indeed. Of course I was as proud as punch, but still struggled to let out feelings and share them even then. Allison insisted they went to Sunday school and this lead to many an argument, where I would exclaim if I was off on a Sunday, I should get to see them and any way, that Christian stuff was crazy! But they went all the same, Allison got her way or should I say looking back, the Lord did.

Allison always tried to encourage me to take part, to drop them off, pick them up or attend carol services etc., but I wasn't having any of it. Anyway, without a doubt I made many mistakes, caused many arguments and behaved less than gentlemanly, yet Allison loved me all the same and time marched on.

For many years before Christ, work took center stage, using 70 hours of my life up every week. The devil sure likes to keep you busy, to keep you not only from God but also from our loved ones and what a good job he did with me. My Job came first along with my results, my achievements, my status, which left other people in last place, no quality time and no time to build "relationships." What hurts the most is this applied to Allison and the Kids more than anyone and I didn't see this until the Lord stepped in.

So life was pretty good for me, it was calm, health was good, finances were good, career was great. Suddenly, one morning, I sat bolt upright in bed and felt driven to get up and ask Allison could we go to church. I just felt I had to go that day, Nov 11th 2007. Yes, I had been working alongside a Christian guy, but certainly had not been given the "hard sell" but could sense something different. Anyway, Allison thought I was being smart and quite rightly said "are you trying to start another fight, if you really want to go, go by yourself." So I did, I just had to!

On April 6th 2008, my whole family went to Church together in the evening. I hadn't attended that often but was giving it a go even though I didn't want to really be there, let's say I was curious. That night the service wafted over me but at the end, I couldn't move from my seat and I wept uncontrollably, the first tears in almost 30 years as I realized the truth. I was confused but I heard my youngest daughter Amber say to her mum, "Dads been saved." I was still rigid in my seat but soaked in tears. Not long after I was shown the prayer list Amber had written asking for my salvation with my name at the top.

From that moment on, I was a new creation. I went home, poured every drop of alcohol down the sink, looked at the world with different eyes and emotion came to life in me. Now bear with me, but at this point, I was on cloud nine, saved, and on my way to a heaven somewhere I thought was made up but not anymore. So what of everyone else? Well I knew my kids were saved at Sunday school and stuff but I never really understood Allison's position. See we didn't discuss it really since University or since I stormed out of a meeting with a minister my wife hoped would marry us. He didn't by the way; we visited Him to ask, and when He told me money was the root of all evil and insisted I read all about it, I wasn't impressed and believed stronger than ever it was all bunkum and left Allison and the minister as I headed to the door.

So back to Allison, my first Christian mission on my salvation was to persuade her to get saved. Her reply was simply "it doesn't work like that Alan!" A few weeks later however, she got held up after church and came out eventually to inform me she "had got right with the Lord," not that she had been saved. I was confused but it turned out she had been saved since a young age and wouldn't upset things because I was so against God. She had actually been praying for me ever since our first debate and simply trusted and believed I was who God wanted her to marry, and that I would in God's time come to Christ!

The Journey, as you will read in my poetry, wasn't easy before Christ and has certainly not been straight forward since. But it has been blessed and worth it all. The first few years after Christ stepped in to my life were easy, everything fell in to place, times were wonderful. But it's then when you come under attack and since then, the family has been struck by serious health issues, grief, employment worries and the evil of self-harm and depression that the devil uses to attack so many people today; took hold of my youngest daughter but impacted the whole family. Here really was something to test our faith!

HOW DEEP IS LOVE

That storm is pretty much over but it serves to remind us how the Christian walk is more like being on a surf board, where sometimes you ride the waves, other times you make mistakes and fall off and on occasion you are hit upside the face by tidal waves from the storms of life.

So, on being saved, God shaped me into becoming a Christian poet by laying words and phrases on my heart. He often leads me to write uncontrollably until a message or a poem is complete. He has used this poetry and its creation to rebuild me to soften my heart to teach me and change my direction.

About 3 years ago I had a vision that my poetry would be laid down in a book to be shared with others. I couldn't make sense of it but I believed it and continued to write as the Lord stirred my heart with His. From day one of my salvation, I have had a burning passion for souls. Not just because my faith tells me to but because on realizing the ultimate truth of Christ and what He has done for me, how He has plucked me from the gates of Hell and given me new life. So knowing this, how could I not want to make myself available to God to do whatever he wishes, no matter how ominous, impossible or ridiculous it sounds or how uncomfortable it may make me feel as my trust is in Him alone.

MY CRY

Give me strength to live!
Give me life to die!
Give me hope forever!
Give me love Today!

How it began

It began as a boy, troubled and broken;
Parental warfare loud and outspoken.
Abused and contested like a powerful commodity;
Emotionally disfigured, I became the neighborhood oddity!

Bullied just as much at home as on the playground floor;
Repeatedly explaining that I'd walked into a door!
Authority in the home I never really had;
Unless of course you mean the drunk, who called himself my dad!

He never was at home that much, he visited at night.
I know that 'cos I wet the bed, when mum and dad would fight.
The longer this went on you see, the colder I became;
Until one day I couldn't feel, love or fear or shame!

Homemade nightmares, imagination running wild;
Impressionable and vulnerable, the weakness of a child!
The knocking of my confidence and the stunting of my growth;
Replaced by a sense of fear that kept me on my toes!

Fond memories of family, I really can't recall;
But I must have had a childhood, 'cos I'm sure I went to school!
This precious time eluded me, used up by someone else,
Growing up with stubbornness, within a living hell!

HOW DEEP IS LOVE

Through my youth I made a pledge, I never would give up;
To soldier on and show the world, I'm made of sterner stuff!
As time went on I thought of ME and nothing else besides;
Selfishly indulging my pleasures and desires.

Then one day an Angel came and saw past all the shame;
Loving me unconditionally, she helped put out the flames.
A mustard seed was planted, deep within my life;
Unbeknown to me, that Angel would become my wife!

We became the best of friends, in love completely true;
A secret marriage made in Heaven, when the Angel said I do.
Still within my mortal coil I believed I'd feed the worms;
Contesting quite religiously, the Christians on MY terms!

As time went on through the years, three more miracles I would have.
Yet still I wasn't convinced by the blessings that called me Dad.
Life moved on and slipped away and still I didn't see;
The risk that I was taking for all eternity!

In control and doing well I gambled with my life;
Knocking on the doors of hell, not knowing the faith of my wife.
For twenty years she prayed for me, trusting in her Lord;
Never doubting that He'd come for me, and arm me with the Sword.

I ONCE WAS HE....

I once was he who did not see;
Driving the nails in Calvary's tree!
A dying man with blinkers on;
No concept of my Fathers Son.

My life was great for it was mine;
Relentlessly towing Satan's line!
Afraid to share or give it up;
The poison chalice I would sup!

Little did I know my life was planned;
My Jesus kept me from being dammed.
In love picked out, before I was made;
Adopted child of God, my soul was saved.

As the ripples of the storm pulsate towards the reeds;
I pray to the one, who always meets my needs!
He silently surrounds me, like the early morning Sun;
Tackling my troubles, until each one is undone.

He wraps His arms around me to let me know He's here;
Although I cannot see Him, He releases all my fear.
He molds me with His love until I am no more;
The shipwreck I've been living in, He guides into the shore.

The enemy encamped around me, starving me of joy;
Feeding on my worries has been his oldest ploy!
Waiting for the winepress, to one day run dry;
Yet, love made me a miracle, when Jesus heard my cry!

A Sense of God

I met a man that I did not see.
He showed me a vision of eternity.
I still cannot believe, that He picked out me;
As by His grace He set me free.

I heard from a man without a sound.
He spoke into my life, turned me around.
I am still amazed at what He had planned;
As I'm standing now on solid ground.

I was touched by a man I could not feel.
He sent His Son, in the ultimate appeal.
I'm still astounded by His power to heal;
Assured my place in Heaven is real.

I walk with a man whose perfume I smell.
He quenches my thirst with a living well.
I'm still aware, that I was bound for hell;
Now Hallelujah! I've good news to tell.

I share His bread daily that I cannot taste.
He sends manna from Heaven that I must not waste.
I'm still in awe that He took my place;
Now I carry my cross and seek His face.

Zephaniah 3:17

The Lord your God is in your midst, a mighty one who will save; he will rejoice over you with gladness; he will quiet you by his love; he will exult over you with loud singing.

THE REAL ME.......

Praying to be the real me, the one not contorted by stress and pain!
The man who can love and express what's inside, without fear or shame!
The father, the husband, the friend and the neighbor.
The man that can bring an open heart and an outlook of favor.

The real me is encased in the shell of the world.
Somewhere within, is the hope of a Pearl.
Locked up by anger, bitterness and fear;
Suffocating the love from the ones I hold dear.

Afraid to reach out in a leap of faith;
The Real me is imprisoned to keep myself safe!
My time in the valley lasted too long;
As I constantly thirsted for the words to my song.

A sinner like David but never so brave;
A wandering sheep that would one day be saved.
So now that I'm singing and my futures secured;
The Real me.....is praying to be more like the Lord!

2 Corinthians 3:18

and we all, who with unveiled faces contemplate the Lords glory, are being transformed into his image with ever increasing glory, which comes from the Lord who is spirit.

A Revelation and Invitation

Oh Lord give me vision and clarity;
Open my eyes to my spiritual reality.
Lead me to the cross, where your will be done;
Onward and upward as I follow your Son.
Mold me and shape me to whom I should be;
My compass aligned to eternity.
A victim of sin saved by your grace;
Given new life, when your Son took my place!
I shall follow the Lamb, for as long as I AM;
The Lord is my Shepherd the 23rd Psalm.
The truth set me free and opened my eyes;
As at once I believed, in total surprise!
A miracle performed on me by the King;
Given new life and a new song to sing.
Adopted in Heaven as a child of my God;
The second my heart cried out to the Lord.
So you see, I am blessed and you'd never have guessed,
That one day to Jesus, my sins I'd confess.

Psalm 51:10 Create in me a pure heart, O God, and renew a steadfast spirit within me.

PARDONED BY THE PRINCE OF PEACE

I have spilled the blood of which I drink
and scarred the beauty on which I now gaze.
My sin drove the nails to the brink;
of death eternal, but He was raised!
His love runs deeper than man-made scars.
Losing the chains with an unending power;
That crafted man and spoke out stars.
He picked me out, his chosen flower;
To be planted in Heaven, before the Rose
of Sharon, who won my soul in the darkest hour.
Now I pour out my soul, to the one who chose,
my sin stained soul to be redeemed.
I can't comprehend what He has done,
I couldn't have dreamed
that I would meet Gods only Son!

Isaiah 9:6 For to us a child is born, to us a son is given, and the government will be on his shoulders. And he will be called Wonderful Counsellor, mighty God, Everlasting Father, Prince of Peace there will be no end.

Selah vie!

As I sit quietly on my own;
I ponder life's meaning, once unknown.
My bygone mind persuaded to take sides;
No longer fears, or runs and hides.

Selah vie.....

You see as time goes by, you must face the truth;
To accept your Lot, or search for proof.
Many resist the evidence, beyond all reasonable doubt!
Seeking to justify, their own way out!

Selah vie.......

It really doesn't matter how hard you try;
As "it is finished!" Was His cry.
Without objection, He relinquished His life on Earth;
That we may receive our heavenly birth.

Selah vie......

He set aside His unbounded power and authority;
Offering to walk with us, into eternity.
As we cast our stones on His perfection,
He converted the cross into resurrection.

Selah vie.....

Binding Himself to our sin and shame;
Not letting go until we came,
To realize His truth within us all.
Body scarred, heartbroken, bleeding out, yet standing tall.

Selah vie......

His tears flowed down from the crystal sea;
Lest we become a cursed fig tree!
His blood ran freely like a crimson tide;
Washing away our sins from deep inside!

Selah vie.....

So as I sit quietly on my own;
I ponder life's meaning once unknown.
My bygone mind persuaded to take sides,
no longer fears......or runs.......or hides.

Praise the Lord.

Psalm 68:19 Praise be to the Lord, to God our Savior, who daily bears our burdens. Selah

BENEATH THE SHADOW OF THE CROSS

Journeying on beneath the shadow of the cross, is not easy.
Selfishly choosing the route that pleases;
Finding the answers, forgetting the reasons.
I am not alone, but I do fly solo,
Believing in myself, tripping on my ego
Landing in my Sin
The pollution we express each time we give in!
Knowing what's right and failing to act;
Is often the problem when turning your back!
He knows we will falter and let Him down,
But still He loves us and gives us a crown.
He doesn't control us or force us to see,
For what more should persuade us that Christ on the tree!
He died there, to show us that He is the WAY
And even rose again to prove He will stay.

"So many times I fall, sometimes further than I can bear, but I thank Jesus that as a child of God, every time I do He catches me."

Alive in Christ

I have been fearfully and wonderfully made!
So precious, that through love I am saved.
Blessed and humble, I wear the Designer's label.
Invited by the King to sup at the Master's table.

Ever to dwell in the house of the Lord.
My cross to carry, but armed with the Sword.
On my mission, I step out in faith;
Trusting His purpose, commissioned with grace.

The beauty of the Lord now draws me on;
As in times of trouble He keeps me strong.
No more shall I fear, or carry the shame,
But forever more I will praise His name!

Psalm 139:14 I will praise thee; for I am fearfully and wonderfully made.

The journey

Lord of all creation;
Release me from temptation.
Strengthen my resolve within,
To overcome the urge to sin.

Right from wrong, I know for sure,
But still my life is far from pure.
I try so hard but still I fall;
When walking straight has been my call.

The devil hides in camouflage,
Setting traps in his mirage.
Satan lures me in, and then he bites,
As I partake in his delights.

Fall I will, along the WAY,
So I'll always stop, to trust and pray.
For if upon the Rock I stand,
He will forever hold me, in His hand.

So as I race unto the Lord;
I'll build my life upon His word.
Ever thankful for His grace,
As on the cross He took my place.

Coming back He soon will be;
To bring back home, the ones set free.
Then as the Saints go marching in;
Eternal praises I will sing!

So with these words I have within;
I stand assured that I'm forgiven.
Amazing Grace how sweet the sound;
Since Jesus called me heaven bound.

Amen.

WALKING WITH THE SHEPHERD

So I'm on my way, I've made a choice,
I took a stand I raised my voice.
I pledged my heart and claimed my faith,
Trusting Jesus who took my place.
The WAY is not easy by yourself,
More than endurance it takes God's help.
So I will let Him raise me, on my knees;
From glory to glory, by degrees.
As I stumble He holds my hand,
Leading me forth to the Promised Land.
So many times my flesh resists,
But His endless love still persists.
As I travel through the stony ground,
I'm no longer lost, but truly found.
From beyond Damascus to Jerusalem;
He removes all fear and man's confusion.
So now the mountain top's in sight,
I can follow His steps into the light.

Mark 9:24 Immediately the boy's father exclaimed, "I do believe; help me overcome my unbelief!"

Leap like the salmon ....

Saved by grace, that's me!
Unchained from my sin and free.
Rescued from death in love,
Drawn to the cross from above.
Covered by mercy and grace,
Secured in the Father's embrace.
Forgiven, redeemed by the Lamb,
Who humbled Himself as a man.
Now inside my black heart's made clean;
As I carry my cross up stream.
Like the salmon, my journey's not easy
But I'll go wherever Christ leads me...........

Romans 12:2 *Do not conform any longer to the pattern of this world, but be transformed by the renewing of your mind. Then you will be able to test and approve what God's will is --His good, pleasing and perfect will.*

BEAUTY AND THE BEAST

Lacking the courage to be herself, infected by the airbrushed plastic generation,
She continuously devours herself, as the only thing she will eat, is a bodily sensation.
Reaching out to perfection of an under rated beauty, to which she's blind,
CARVING out the imagery, she detests in her mind.
Lost in the snares of the wannabe and the porcelain princess;
She argues her case, in a tantrum of violent illusion and stress.
Slowly becoming obese on the lies of the world, but losing the weight of her worth.
Infatuated by a fantasy of an obsessive and perilous poisonous curse.
Her beauty continues to shine, behind the lies and the counterfeit crowds,
As those that love her, underline the extent to which they're proud.
Encouragement and praise, serve only to unsettle and harass;
As she runs for cover in the maze of the chat room, and the social underclass.
Generating followers, longing to be Liked, of a similar disposition;
Seducing her lust for the benefits, believed to come with malnutrition.
In time the peer group paparazzi leads to a form of bodily vandalism,
Self-inflicted evidence of an irrational coping mechanism.
Hurting herself to feel better, becomes her world's worst kept secret;
A taboo not for attention but an outlet for her suffering, a controllable way to release it.
The method of choice, used as a voice, was to CUT her way out of the pain,
But the relief is only short lived, as the scars only lead to more shame.
Amazing as all this may seem, she lives this alongside a dream,
Not to be the center of attention or some mythical beauty Queen.
Quite simply she wants to escape, from the nightmares of worry and strife,
Embedded in her formative years, by those who surrounded her life.
This conundrum is layered with trouble, as our princess can't plan her

escape;
But with love and unlimited treasure, day by day her life will reshape.
The breakable beauty within us, can so easily shatter and crumble;
As the vessel we live in is fragile, and the pedestal's certain to tumble.
When broken and shattered in pieces, displayed as a trophy in Hell;
Surely it serves as a warning, to the lies of the world's fairy tale.
So build up your children in Love, and open your heart to their cries,
May you ever be eager to Crown them, let this be a word to the wise!

John 10:10 The thief comes only to steal kill and destroy.........

1 Peter 3:3-4 Do not let your adorning be external ----the braiding of hair and the putting on of gold jewelry, or the clothing you wear ---but let your adorning be the hidden person of the heart with the imperishable beauty of a gentle and quiet spirit, which in God's sight is very precious.

Trich or treat:

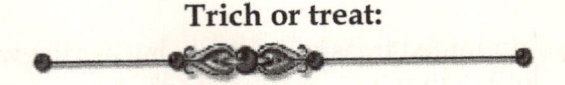

Tugging, pulling, hauling, twisting,
Yanking, prising, jerking, wrenching.
I just can't help my Trichotillomania!
It's obsessive, it's compulsive, it's embarrassing behavior!
I try to keep its existence hidden underneath my hat
Metaphorically speaking that is, as it's not so nice to look at.
Suffering in silence but screaming in my mind.
Compulsively extracting, one by one, each single hair at a time.
Clumps, patches, balding and disfigured,
Somebody help me and tell me how it's triggered!
Hairs, bristles, curls, frizz, fuzz, my crowning glory;
Lock stock and barrel every single one, tells a story.
Forelock, mane, quiff, ringlet and thatch,
Repeatedly resulting in the trophy, of another bald patch.
From my scalp, my arms, my legs, or even from my eyes.
The root to satisfying this itch came as a surprise!
It's out it's out at last the itch is gone,
But now I'm scarred with guilt and shame and need to put my wig on.
I can't believe I've done such harm to every single follicle;
This condition that has grown in me, is simply diabolical.
Grow back! Grow back! Now that would be a feat.
This torment that lives inside of me, is one of Trich or treat!

Psalms 118:8 It is better to trust in the LORD than to put confidence in man.

Proverbs 3:5 Trust in the Lord with all your heart and lean not on your own understanding;

THE WILES OF THE DEVIL

Depression is like hell reaching out the cords of Sheol, to ensnare your joy.
It smothers you in darkness, where hopelessness has always been its ploy.
This melancholic misery comes in many guises,
Devious and subtle, with a style to fit all sizes.

It plays upon your deepest fears,
Branding the heart and drying up tears.
It works upon your soul, suffocating hope,
Tempting your escape, with just the right amount of rope.

The self-righteous and La-di-da's, may mock this torment, quoting "it's all in the mind!"
Quite right, these foolish folk are not far wrong, yet to the truth they're blind.
This cruel and ignorant sarcasm, just serves to escalate the gloom.
Then before you know it, you judge yourself with nothing else but doom.

It's not a game my friend, this battle in your head is real,
Where reckless behaviors manifest themselves, from the emotions that you feel.
Clinically it feeds itself, wearing you away;
Detaching you from reality, in the form of Groundhog Day.

You want to end the nonsense, to free yourself from pain,
But the enemy brings urges, to hurt yourself again and again and again!
Many of us have journeyed here, if the truth be told.
Struggling with our happiness, as our hearts grew cold.

There is more to this than meets the eye, if you look beyond yourself.
Reaching out in faith, to the only source of help.
With courage and nothing else to lose, be bold and touch His robe.
For if you trust in Jesus Christ, you'll be restored like Job.

I understand your heavy heart, will contest this message I convey.
Yet there is living proof, for the reasons that I pray.
So don't let this cloak define your destiny,
But grasp it with both hands, and overcome the enemy!

2 Samuel 22:6-7 NKJV The sorrows of Sheol surrounded me; The snares of death confronted me. In my distress I called upon the Lord, and cried out to my God; He heard my voice from His temple, and my cry entered His ears.

From Crystal meth to Crystal Sea

From Crystal meth to Crystal sea,
The love of Christ will set you free.
From all time low to Heavenly High,
The love of Christ will never die.
From Asouza Street, to streets of Gold,
The love of Christ can save your soul.
From angel dust; to dust to dust,
The love of Christ for all to trust.
From broken homes to broken chains,
The love of Christ, forever reigns.
From Genesis to Revelation,
The love of Christ brings true Salvation.

Amen

HOODWINKED BY HELL!

There are no true Atheists, I do believe;
Only those temporarily deceived.
They take the bait that Satan casts;
Then deny the Lord with hardened hearts.
From time to time, we've all been there;
Tempted in to the Liars Lair!
Doubting Thomas and trusting chance,
As the devil leads a merry dance.
Dressed to kill and HOT to trot!
Creation's truth is soon forgot.
As time goes on and life runs out;
The Atheist will start to Doubt.
There are no true Atheists, of that I'm sure!
Just those too late for Heaven's door!

Psalm 14:1
The fool says in his heart, "There is no God."

Satan's Drug of Choice – Sin

He's a pusher and a dealer
An illegal habit feeder.
A user and abuser
A tempter and confuser.
Giving you the needle, an addict to your pain;
Injecting you with poison and gripping you with shame.
Hooking you on pleasures that you really shouldn't touch.
Soon you will depend on it and use it as a crutch.
Everyone on earth today, will face the poacher's snare;
Believing it in innocence, then hunted everywhere.
Lustfully it kisses you, with the overdose it gives,
While stubbornly you reject the rehab that God gives.
Eventually you're numb and nothing satisfies,
Lost searching for a fix within the web of lies.
You wonder if it's over, if there's an end in sight.
As the devil watches over you, like a thief in the night.
You try to go cold turkey and do it by yourself.
But Satan just keeps teasing you and courting you to hell.
The infections taking over, it spreads from heart to soul,
As the eternal terrorist gets nearer to his goal.
There is a hope for this perilous disease,
Just put your trust in Jesus and watch as Satan flees.
The savior that you needed brings an eternal high,
Covering your tracks as on the cross He died.
Born again forever, brings an endless rush;

As Satan is defeated and beneath your feet is crushed!
No longer bound by the torment that Sin brings,
Instead restored in love by the Mighty King of Kings!
Satan's put on ice and your black heart is now clean,
Worshipping the one who loves you, as by grace you're redeemed!

1 Peter 5:8 Be alert and of sober mind. Your enemy the devil prowls around like a roaring lion looking for someone to devour.

PRAYER

Prayer is not a religious speech or a public recital.
Prayer is the connection to God that is vital.
A direct line to the Father that will never be closed.
A timeless connection through the one that arose.
Never engaged, or "leave a message after the tone"
Immediate reception with the one on the throne.
Not via Facebook, twitter or text;
But by the WAY of the CROSS, at the savior's request.
Pray in the spirit and not in the flesh,
As the answer to prayer is certain to bless.

Philippians 4:6-7 Do not be anxious about anything, but in every situation, by prayer and petition, with thanksgiving, present your requests to God. And the peace of God, which transcends all understanding, will guard your hearts and your minds in Christ Jesus.

How to Pray

How to pray, what to say
Out loud confident and proud.
Where no one sees, on your knees, alone without the crowd.
A personal appointment, a meeting with the King,
Exclusive recognition that death has lost its sting.
V.I.P. attention as Jesus hears your call.
Nothing that we ask of Him is ever far too small.
Millions of voices call out to Him each day.
Not one word goes un-noticed, he hears everything we say.
Face down or arms out stretched, reaching to the sky.
The beauty of our Jesus is, He heeds our every cry.
Not forsaken or forgotten, avoided or ignored,
But mercifully forgiven, through the grace of the Lord.
He longs to hear your call as he listens to your heart.
Surely you remember, He has loved you from the start.

Thessalonians 15:17 Pray without ceasing.

PRAY....

Teach me to pray Lord, to call out from my heart;
To focus my eyes on your glory, knowing you loved me from the start.
Help me to share how I'm feeling,
To lay all that I have at your feet.
Give my life new meaning, as I approach the judgement seat.
Strengthen my path when I'm straying and chasten my tolerance of sin.
While others around me are praying, your spirit is working within!

1 Chronicles 16:11 Seek the LORD and his strength, seek his face continually.

My Prayer

Lord load my pen with Your mighty Word,
And let your precious blood flow a Cross my page.
Whisper in my ear, what shall be heard,
So that those who read, would bring You Praise.
Quicken my heart with the old, old, story.
As the author of my Salvation, Lord live in me,
So that I may tell of your grace and Glory
Giving others a glimpse of eternity.

FATHER....

Guide my steps along the way,
Soften my heart so I will always pray,
As I grow old upon the earth,
May I never forget how much souls are worth.
Give me strength to plough the field,
And in your presence may I be still.
As I journey deeper towards the Son,
Grant me grace to soldier on.
Until the day you call me home,
May I always let your love be known.

The hope of glory

I pray the world will see in me,
a reflection of eternity.
I pray the look upon my face,
will display your saving grace.
I pray the words and things I do,
will testify my love for you.

Colossians 1:27 To them God has chosen to make known among the Gentiles the glorious mystery, which is Christ in you the hope of glory.

RELIGION

Religion; it's a man-made illusion;
A weapon of the devils confusion.
A publicly censored way to believe.
A smoke screen from Satan that won't let you breathe.

Military style rules of engagement,
When marriage is merely a sexual arrangement.
A code of conduct to keep you in line;
Not to focus you on Jesus divine.

A Sunday appointment that's rarely been kept,
Instead of a grateful commitment, because Jesus Wept!
A cross worn for fashion, to accessorize,
Rather than proclaiming the King is alive!

Denominational arguments on what's right or wrong,
When we should all be united in a new song!
Wickedly induced rules and regulations,
Ignorantly serving to separate congregations.

Terminal entrapment by religious dominions,
Creating seasonal believers and ceremonial Christians!
The antidote's eternal, it's always at hand,
Simple faith believing, in the form of a man.

Christian G.P.S. that guides us when we pray,
While religion leads us nowhere and distracts us from the WAY!
Faith's spiritual adrenaline, injected by His grace,
A catalyst for Salvation, if you demonstrate your Faith.

Religion comes from Man and must always be obeyed.
While faith comes from the cross where true love was displayed,
An open invitation to whosoever believes.
When born again in Jesus, religion disappears!

We all do it!

We all do it, we judge and opinionate!
We focus on the outside, the superficial and the things that fascinate!
We don't see real beauty, just what pleases us!
The short term pleasure that stimulates and teases us.

It doesn't last, it's away in a FLASH; like a SHOT from a gun!
Too wrapped up in the meaningless and selfishness we always come undone.
Yet, when we were children, our hearts were open wide.
Then as the poison of the serpent filtered through the world, our hearts hardened inside.

We didn't feel the changing of the guard around our hearts,
As ever since Eden, we've been tempted by lustful body parts.
Many say beauty is in the eye of the beholder,
If that's the truth, then pluck it out before we get much colder!

We see it every day, the bitterness within,
Sugar coated experiences that sweeten every SIN!
Adrenaline, dopamine and endorphins may satisfy the mind.
While men collect their wages from HELL, as Satan makes them blind.

It's not as if we were not warned or taught the WAY to go.
Yet Satan rewards our sin with that warm and fuzzy feeling that's kindled down below.
As we warm our sleight of hands on the devil's charms
We forget we should be LEANING, LEANING in His everlasting arms....

At this point of tolerance my friend, man's ugliness is reflected.
But there's hope for everyone that this plague has infected.
Now this vaccine; this antidote to HELL; it's not something you can purchase or consume Within a shake!
It's an ETERNAL heart transplant, a GIFT from Jesus, not some decision that you make.

It's a matter of belief and surrendering one's SOUL
As you no longer thirst or hunger, when you let the MASTER take control.
Resist you may, saying it's not for you right now, this spiritual kind of thing.
So my friend I leave you with just a single verse and that's John 3:16

LET EVERY DAY BE SUNDAY

Sometimes the Sunday service can become the Sunday show!
Preaching to the converted who no longer want to know!
Dressed in their finest to say they're well to do,
Claiming their rightful place within the social pew.
Observing all around them, critiquing what was said,
No longer really hearing the message in the bread.
When it comes to worship, they shuffle through the songs choosing what to sing,
Forgetting that their worship is destined for the King.
Distracted by the world, the meeting rushes by,
you'd think from some reactions, that the well had just run dry.
See this is man's religion, not the freedom to which we're called.
If only we would trust in our conviction and rejoice in the Lord.
Only then will the show be over and the true service begin,
And we'll overflow with worship as we truly live in Him.
Our hearts will sing like David and our souls will seek His face,
As we truly follow Jesus and the beauty of His grace.
So each day be sure to give Him your Sunday best,
For this is more than an expression of the WAY that we should dress.
Lift up your arms and praise Him, sing glory to His name,
Let every day be Sunday and never be the same...

Pull up the pews help build the church

A different seat in church are you serious!
"We've been sitting here for years, minding our own business and now you dare to sit near us!"
When I sat among them, I struggled to see Jesus!
Having descended from the balcony, I wondered if they feared us...
"It's just not the same these days, so many strangers visit church."
"The songs aren't what they used to be, I don't even know the words!"
"I give every week you know, my envelope is full!"
"I've been coming here for years I even went to Sunday school!"
"MY Church is NICE You see, it's always been the same!"
"But now they're inviting everyone, that JESUS, He's to blame."

Too often church is closed, as if it's become exclusive.
How can we forget salvations free and for none it is elusive.
It's time we looked outside and opened wide our arms.
Inviting everyone we CROSS and woo them with the Psalms.
For if the church is Holy, no walls will keep folks out.
We must all sit down together and worship without doubt!

Romans 15:7
Therefore accept one another just as Christ also accepted us to the glory of God.

IGNORANCE IS BLISS

Ignorance is bliss,
Or is it Satan's kiss;
Deceiving you of life
So you will not count the price.
Courting you to hell,
Without that burning smell,
Until one day you stand alone;
Weighed down by sin, you once condoned!
That's how the story goes, if you choose to turn away;
Ignoring all the warning signs that God has sent your way!
Like the old lady's "thank you Son, God bless"
Or the teacher back in school, who said "own up now, come on confess!"
The gospel tracts you cast aside;
Or the battle with your conscience, from which you couldn't hide!
Whatever way you cut it, the story's getting told;
Either one of victory, or the losing of your soul!
Matthew, Mark, Luke and John, lived to tell the truth,
And Jesus Christ did everything, so that you would have the proof!
I'm not making this up! I've been there before myself,
Playing Russian roulette, first with Heaven and then with Hell!
The over whelming evidence, presented all before;
Suddenly made sense, the day I met the Lord!

Ephesians 4:18 Having the understanding darkened, being alienated from the life of God through the ignorance that is in them, because of the blindness of their heart.

More than a book

My Bible's not just a book, it's the WORD
A message that will not go UNHEARD
It's a guide, it's the truth, it's the WAY
My Bible's not heavy, it's the LIGHT
It's surely not dead, it's the LIFE
(as long as it's not buried away)
My Bible's not history it's a PRESENT
A gift to the world and a KEY
Unlocked by the savior, God SENT
To secure our ETERNITY
My Bible's not long, it's ETERNAL
Everlasting and true to the END
A love letter from ABBA PATERNAL
To whom one day I'll ASCEND

1 Peter 1:25 But the word of the Lord remains forever. "And this word is the good news that was preached to you.

SO!

So many lessons yet to be learned.
So much respect that cannot be earned.
So much love, that longs to be shared.
So many reasons, for man to be scared.
So many problems, that need to be solved,
While so many people, are losing their souls!
So many starving that need to be fed,
While so many refuse, their daily bread!
So many excuses for things left undone
And so many children, needing the SON.
So many struggling and losing their WAY!
As so many found, fall down and pray!
So few are willing and ready to give,
As many cold hearted, are warmed to resist.
So many times he calls us back home,
While those that refuse Him, will only hear groans.
So will you respond and accept His Grace,
While Jumping for joy and leaping in faith.

Passion for Souls

Indifference is tragic when it comes to life or death.
Especially as man keeps on sinning, until his final breath.
Immune to the gospel, no matter how clear it's truth,
Ignoring God's message until they see real proof.

If only they would listen before the judgement day,
And put their trust in Jesus, for He's the only WAY.
So do you see your purpose of your Christian life on earth,
It's to reach out to the lost with everything your worth.

Do the tears roll down your face,
When you smell that fiery place?
Do you hunger for salvation,
To descend upon our nation?

If the answer to God's Leading is to act upon His call,
Be sure that you answer Him, and give to Him your all!
The time is running out, as souls just slip away
And the harvest is among us, as Jesus hears us PRAY

Step out of life's boat and begin your Heavenly mission,
With a passion now for Souls, it's time we started fishing!

TIME FOR CLEAN HEARTS AND DIRTY HANDS

I pray these words turn the tables in the temple of your mind,
Shaking free the scales that so often make us blind.

Speaking as a Christian, it's time we told the truth,
Living out our faith with a testimony of proof.
We all fall short and sin, let's be honest about it!
The blessing is in the brokenness, we struggle to admit.

We're not as bright as we think, as it's Christ who shines in us,
As we portray an image that we'd never even "cuss"
Now that's a lie implied by our ego and our piety,
Misleading our faith in the eyes of society.
We are certainly not perfect, but Christ is, in us,
transforming our lives, if in Him we place our trust.

Yet we pretend to be blessed, in a host of popular ways.
Eloquently speaking of them, as everybody prays.
Raising our hands in church and singing every chorus,
As the multitudes outside "get lost" right before us.

You see man looks on the outward, while God looks on the heart,
And we must not conform and live life "a la Carte."
So hunger for His presence, and He will feed us manna;
If we trust in Him for everything, as faithfully as Hannah.

As Christians we stumble, a few steps forward, a few steps back;
Almost bragging that we can resist the enemy's attack!
Yet the grace of God restores us, when we do the things we hate,
As each of us is tempted by the smell of Satan's bait.

God sees the secrets of our hearts and all our indiscretions,
But chooses in His mercy to blot out all of our transgressions.
Surely this should teach us the WAY that we should go.
Have we not learned a thing since the walls of Jericho!

The ways of man are foolish and the ways of God seem strange.
Still He cancels out our sin, and not in part exchange.
So speaking as His children, it's time we told the truth,
Warning the multitudes of Hell, while the sanctimonious see this
uncouth!

All of us still sin, now let's be honest about this!
Lest we deceive ourselves before the Lord, like Ananias.
Before we make disciples, we must first prepare ourselves,
For many reject Jesus, as believers sentence them to Hell!

We must surely destroy the lumber yard within our clouded eyes;
Removing every splinter to our enemies' surprise.
We must lead with love and reach out with holy hands,
Sharing with humility and a heart that understands.

You see, none of us are righteous, no, not even one.
Yet the truth will set us free and His will it will be done!
So as the temperature is rising and the heat is on,
Why not fan the flames within you and be a witness just like John.

I pray these words will turn the tables in the temple of your mind,
Shaking free the scales that so often make us blind.

Matthew 23:26 Blind Pharisee: First clean the inside of the cup and the dish, and then the outside also will be clean.

Armed and Ready for the Clarion Call

We have been enlisted in the army of the Lord,
To fend off evil, armed with power of the sword!
Marching into battle with Angels on our shoulders,
Raising up legions of convicted Christian soldiers.

To convey His love is our Pentecostal mission,
With the courage of Peter and John, our great commission.
Under the cover of Christ, for all to see,
Proclaiming the gospel to set the captives free.

Prepared for combat with prayer and the shedding of tears,
From Genesis to Revelation and beyond all man's frontiers,
Setting our faces like flint and like Gideon enter the fray,
Putting on our Armor, until that glorious day.

Defend the 50th day with an all-consuming fire,
Ever covered by His blood, surrendering to the Holy spirits desire.
We may not have been in the Upper Room, on the birthday of the
Church.
Yet until the Trumpet sounds, we must set about His work.

We will be injured by the first stones of an unbelieving nation,
Confronted by His wounded side, with doubt placed there by Satan.
Hallelujah! Through the blood we have gained the victory,
As Acts of Pentecostal power are true for you and me!

*Acts 1:8 But ye shall receive power, after that the Holy Ghost is come upon you:
and ye shall be witnesses unto me both in Jerusalem, and all Judea, and in
Samaria, and unto the uttermost part of the earth.*

WHAT DO YOU SEE?

Christian, look around you, what do you see?
Do you see the prisoner struggling to break free?
What about the broken hearted searching for peace,
or the tormented sinner longing for release!

Christian, have you heard the cries of the lonely
and the screaming of the demons hunting for trophies?
Then there's the weeping and wailing of those setting courses like Jonah,
bragging to the world behind an Atheist persona!

Believer, do you truly have the courage of your conviction?
Do you not mean the words you utter, when you pray the benediction!
There is no fear in love, so where is your boldness to proclaim?
Please do not sit in church and procrastinate if evangelism is your aim.

Brothers and sisters, time is short and there's no promise of our
tomorrows;
except for Christ, when His grace He bestows,
as He speaks peace on a new creation.
Only in this moment are sins forgiven, through the gift of our salvation.

Disciples, have you not forsaken all you had,
surrendered wholly to Him, rejoiced and been glad?
Please do not fall asleep as the hour gets late,
but plough on with every dying breath and celebrate.

Saints, can you hear me, have I not truth in my heart?
Have you really grown so weary of "How Great Thou Art?"
Surely when the storm is over and you hear the Church bells ring,
you will keep marching on eternally, in honor of the King!

Jeremiah 1:13 The word of the Lord came to me again: What do you see?
"I see a pot that is boiling," I answered. "It is tilting towards us from the north."

The Crux of the Matter

The cross,
standing;
raised upright;
calling us.
Nails, hammered;
wrought iron,
His will;
breaking
chains.
His bones;
unbroken,
prophecy in action.
Heart open;
blood;
pumping;
freely given,
as eternity pauses;
death trembled;
beaten;
arose, among thorns;
twisted;
soldiers;
crowned the King of Kings;
selfless,
immense in mercy,
killing, sin.
Skin,
whipped, ripped;
hangs;
in ribbons,
cut;
above;

darkness falling,
stars;
written in,
bloody sweat
and tears.
Jesus wept;
over Jerusalem;
city;
of God,
given forgiveness.
My freedom;
won;
His mission;
accomplished.
Salvations plan;
fulfilled;
on a tree;
at Calvary.

Luke 23:33 When they came to the place called the Skull, they crucified Him there along with the criminals one on His right, the other on His left.

HE WILL NEVER LEAVE ME......................

I have been away a while,
Trapped within the confines of this open space.
Temporarily distracted by the world and its smile,
Almost forgetting the wonder of His grace.

Forgive me father, for going it alone;
Paddling my own canoe, drifting toward the rocks.
Putting on hold the sacrifice you've shown,
Caught within the currents, not clinging to the cross.

I didn't stop believing, I just had to get things done!
Succumbing to the trappings of the net cast upon the world,
Instead of living first in search of the Son,
Trusting in His promises adopted as His child.

So now that I have wandered and fended for myself;
I have learned how much He loves me, as He kept me within His hand.
Marching on my ego, I knocked the doors of Hell!
But this was just a snare, and not what God had planned.

So now like the prodigal, I run into His arms,
Harvesting the mustard seed, planted in my soul.
I surrender all to Jesus, relinquish worldly charms.
I have decided! I have decided! That Jesus makes me whole!

Oh what a faithful God.

Isaiah 30:21 Whether you turn to the right or to the left, your ears will hear a voice behind you saying, "This is the way; walk in it."

Abba father

Tonight I will tell you of the one, of whom, you have all heard.
One who's name goes far beyond any three letter word!
Many of you will know Him and have called upon His name,
Yet some of you still wonder if He deserves His fame.

Too often I hear men say His name is just a myth, something Christians feel.
I'm here as living proof that my ABBA FATHER is absolutely real.
He introduced Himself to me when I least expected,
Now having acknowledged Him, I'm eternally protected.

His name! I hear you say, that you've heard this all before.
If that were true my friend, would you really have come through the door?
Bear with me just a little longer, as I tell you of His name.
I cannot sum Him up or put Him in a box, but His praises I will proclaim!

He began as Elohim and in the beginning was the Word.
The Alpha and Omega, King of kings, and Lord of Lords!
He is the ONE who sees me, my provider and my healer, His name reflects this all.
He is my everlasting father, my redeemer and my friend who met me as with Paul.

You see, His name is not like mine that tells you what to call me!
It's a reflection of His love for us, an everlasting glory.
His name is the essence of His majesty and all sustaining power.
Hallowed be thy name I pray, a sacred gentle flower.

In the beginning was the word and to Moses, the Great I AM.
To you and me He's everything, the first, the last, the lamb.
We can choose to resist His name or curse it until we die!
But eventually His sovereign name is the only one you will cry!

Now this is where it all gets real and there's business to be done.
You see, His name was made flesh in the form of His only son,
Where calling on the power of His name comes true Salvation.
Whatever way you dress this up my friends, His name is Jesus Christ, in
any translation!

Acts 4:12 And there is salvation in no one else, for there is no other name under Heaven given among men by which we must be saved.

EMET-TRUTH

Do you really believe the Bible? I was asked.
Jesus walked on water! The sceptic laughed!
How can you believe what clearly sounds so daft;
That a man brought fourth water from a rock, with a staff!
Why Mr. Atheist, are you so easily offended by the thought of my God
and King?
Religiously offended by the notion of, well; simply nothing!
Refusing to meet Christ, sincerely leaves me weeping,
As gnashing of teeth may one day be your greeting.
I must admit, I once myself wore your shoes;
Stumbling through the darkness, trying so hard to disprove,
The very existence of the creator, as proclaimed by the Jews!
Until a divine appointment surprised my unbelief, through Eternity's
good news.
So you may fight the miraculous like the centurion day by day,
But you cannot hide the visible from the invisibles WAY!
No matter how pleasing the pattern of the world's cabaret;
Saul became Paul and the truth is here to stay.

Romans 1:20 For since the creation of the world God's invisible qualities--his eternal power and divine nature--have been clearly seen, being understood from what has been made, so that people are without excuse.

Cosmic Soup or Holy Proof

Big Bang Theory, evolution!
They're all so sure, but nothing's proven!
Scientific evidence,
lacking only common sense.
From the sea came you and me?
Wisdom based on lunacy!

If this were true we'd see it now,
We'd see a sheep become a cow!
Things would randomly appear,
If there was nothing and now I'm Here!

A house needs a builder, an effect needs a cause,
Like a bird needs the wind and a cat needs its paws.
Creation isn't random, it's clearly by design.
It's obviously miraculous and points to one divine.

A baby needs a mother,
A sister needs a brother.
The chicken or the egg you ask, you cannot pick them both!
For if you did, then scrambled eggs could peck you on the nose!

Don't be silly, don't be daft you say,
There's more to life than meets the eye, we're learning more each day.
But to learn we need a teacher, the one who knows it all,
That's why I believe in Jesus, since I returned His call.

So if you look around you, you're sure to see the proof,
Of our Heavenly creator, whose creation tells the TRUTH!

Romans 1:20 For since the creation of the world God's invisible qualities--his eternal power and divine nature---have been clearly seen, being understood from what has been made, so that people are without excuse.

IF ONLY ....

If you knew that tomorrow wouldn't come,
Would you change?
If your heart beat stopped and your time was done,
Would your next move be the same?

If death was just a breath away and you could taste it,
Would it be bitter as you say goodbye?
Maybe if you didn't know, you'd carry on, not having to admit;
Your final destination is burning for you, until the day you die!

If you realized the measure of your life on earth was closing;
Would you make your peace?
Would you extend the hand of friendship to those you've been opposing?
Would the fighting cease?

If you knew before the week was up, your loved ones would pass away,
Do you think that you would love them more?
Possibly as the tide went out, you would wet your feet and pray,
Lovingly and faithfully guiding them to the shore!

If the opportunity to speak again, was taken from your lips;
Would you regret the things you should have said?
Would you savor the moments or rewrite the script?
Playing out what could have been, before you end up dead!

If you stopped to evaluate the present in your hand;
Would you choose to believe?
Would you accept the things you cannot see and do not understand?
Would you recognize eternity, and to Jesus would you cleave?

If you knew that tomorrow wouldn't come;
Would you change?
Would you lift your hand in worship and call upon the Son?
Would your next move be the same ....

Mustard and miracles

Man sees miracles as what he can't conceive,
Something greater than one could ever possibly believe.
Surely the mind of man could not have imagined what it sees today,
So therefore miracles have gone before and so must be here to stay!

Unbelief and disbelief are negative in nature;
Simply putting off what one will find out later!
Proving what exists right now does not explain the cause.
In fact the atheist needs faith, and that's his fatal flaw.

You see life begets life, but where does it begin?
Whatever way you look at things, it starts and ends with sin!
You justify your way of life by what you choose to do.
Not by weighing up the evidence, or based on what is true!

So when you look into the eyes of a new born child;
Or hold the hand and meet the eyes of a loved one who's just died.
Surely you can't tell me it's all a big mistake,
A scientific coincidence and that my God's a fake!

For if you truly looked upon the living and the dead,
Surely you would see beyond the windows in their head.
In one you see the life poured out by the eternal soul,
The other one is vacant, no longer inhabited, no longer whole.

So believe it or not, you live inside a shell;
Destined one day for Heaven, or is it Hell!
You cannot tell me it does not cross your mind,
Just look into the mirror and tell me what you find!

I know it's not always that easy to believe!
If it was, then it would be so easy to conceive,
To have conjured up the world and everything we see.

But then again who on earth would have created you and me?

A chemical explosion, a physical mystery.
A timeless existence prior to HIS-STORY.
If knowledge and science can prove how life began,
Then how is it that science requires something more than man?

In the beginning was the WORD, nothing or something has to be your choice!
Nothing is a miracle and something gives you a voice.
So as miracles you can't believe then something created us!
Surely then you must believe that's miraculous, and a little faith's enough!

Luke 18:27 Jesus replied, "What is impossible with man is possible with God."

MAJESTICAL WORSHIP

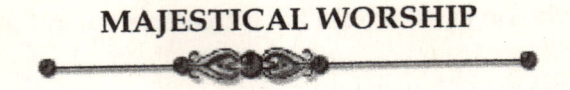

Shining in the firmament, like a cosmic flame;
The universe speaks the beauty of His holy name.
Infinity dare not come close to the measure of His love
That wraps around existence like a velvet glove.

His power cannot be contained in the expanse of time or space,
For every atom that "matters," worships Him in this place.
The planets they obey Him and the stars they dance,
Even Mother Nature sings in praise at every chance.

The sun and moon compare Him together;
Reflecting His majesty in the heavens forever.
Shooting stars display themselves in gestures to the beauty of His
sacrifice;
As an act of revelation to our future hope of paradise.

Even Saturn adorns a thousand rings in devotion to eternity;
As both Heaven and earth are summoned to bear witness to Love's
identity.
Above the circle of the earth hangs an unbounded labyrinthine tapestry,
Dedicated to the tabernacle for the myriad of galaxies.

Upon the Earth the Psalmist sang, "the earth be glad the sea resound,"
"the skies proclaim His handiwork" as with glory He is crowned.
In His presence mountains quake and oceans roar;
While His voice strikes like lightning to the 1st 2nd and 3rd encore!

Soon one day the Sun will fade and the moon itself, dim down,
As the stars cry holy, giving way to the Lord's renown.
The heavens will disappear, consumed for all to see;
As the myriads of angels sing worthy, worthy is He.

Psalm 8:1-2 O Lord, our Lord, how majestic is your name in all the earth! You have set your glory above the Heavens.

Revelation of joy

Joy comes with the breaking of each new day;
Like the sun smiling as it rises over the bay.
Nature preaches God's existence, as it worships in His cathedral;
Proclaiming his might and power, giving us wings like the eagle.

Relentlessly proposing in silence from heaven that we cannot see.
Yet every man can hear him as he displays his majesty.
Even in the darkness, the SON will surely shine;
As David introduces us to our God divine.

JOY is in his glory, it's everywhere you look;
The WAY to receiving it is written in his book.
Trust upon his word and you will know Him as your Lord,
As he arms you with wisdom and the power of the sword.

Follow his directions and he will make your ways straight;
If you will see him in your heart before it is too late.
He will guide you from the valley, unto the mountain top;
If you will simply follow him and vow to never stop.

JOY can be unspeakable, but tell of it you must,
For keeping it a secret would surely be unjust.
The treasure of his kingdom is priceless to the soul;
More valuable than pearls, more profitable than gold.

Psalm 19 v1
The heavens declare the glory of God, the skies proclaim the work of his hands.

ETERNALLY GRATEFUL

This could be your final day;
But for my Lord I'm ready come what may.
My trust is in His yesterday, the same today, forever!
So I will lift my eyes to Him,
My eternal, risen treasure.

Creation stares at men, its truth so clear and sure;
A self portrait of love, behind Heaven's open door.
Painted in the Artist's blood,
The unique signature of God.
A masterpiece of His perfection;
He raised the Standard through His resurrection.

This miracle I now contain;
As by His blood I'm born again!
Blackened by sin I tried to deny!
I questioned the Gospel with WHAT? HOW? And WHY?

Then with mercy and grace my Lord set me free;
When I finally accepted my King on that tree.
Now I'm on a journey that's Heaven bound.
I pray you will join me if your faith can be found!!

Leave your sins far behind you;
Take His hand, climb aboard.
Let His blood set you free,
Then put your trust in the Lord.

Psalm 105:1 Oh give thanks to the Lord; call upon his name; make known his deeds among the peoples!

"Simply remembering Billy, a man who accepted the Lord before it was too late, a man whose smile was as big as his heart. Still trusting the Lord for household salvation."

Calvary's Tapestry

As my Lord reached down to earth to save His people,
He was already threading my life, through the eye of the needle.
Traversing eternity with outstretched arms;
That one day my praises would out-sing the Psalms.
While giving up His life at Calvary;
My savior was already weaving love's tapestry.
Taking my rags and washing them clean;
Clothing me like Joseph, with things unseen.
Knit one "pearl," one of the greatest price;
Spinning my story; swifter than the weavers shuttle, on the loom of life!
While soldiers divided his clothes and cast lots;
Only clothing us in righteousness, was in His thoughts.
Offering up His spirit, the veil was torn;
As it was finished, I was being reborn.
Three hours of darkness as black as Onyx;
Then the father's feelings were made known in the earth's tectonics.
The very fabric of time was now marked......forever.
Offering the seal of Christ to the whosoever.

John 19:30 When he had received the drink, Jesus said, "It is finished." With that he bowed his head and gave up his spirit.

IN HIM

In Him there is no condemnation!
No punishment or retaliation,
No judging voice or discrimination,
No bitterness or retribution,
No natural selection or denomination.

In Him there is no condemnation!
No exclusive club or separation,
No secret word or combination,
No test to pass or indoctrination,
No fee to pay or initiation.

In Him there is no condemnation!
No point to prove or humiliation,
No charge to face or accusation,
No time to serve or incarceration,
No death penalty or castigation.

In Him there is true Salvation!
Amazing grace and redemption,
A new beginning a transformation,
Release from sin, exoneration,
A child of God a new creation,
Set apart in sanctification.

In Him there is true Salvation!
A place in Heaven what jubilation,
Adopted by Christ in justification,
A king to worship in adoration,
Holy, holy eternal congregation.

Celebration! Celebration! Celebration!

Romans 8:1
Therefore, there is now no condemnation for those who are in Christ Jesus, because through Christ Jesus the law and the Spirit of life set me free from the law of sin and death.

In His Arms

Upon the cross, He hung for me.
Arms outstretched to set me free.
For many years in the past,
Until one day He touched my heart.

Calling, crying, pleading in pain,
Arms wide open, my salvation to claim.
Overwhelmed by His love, my burdens released,
Now His gospel's within me, my ignorance ceased.

My eyes have been opened, the truths become clear.
In His arms now forever I've nothing to fear.
Surrendered to Jesus my life is secure,
Washed in His blood so powerful and pure.

He died in my place and poured out His love,
Birthing forgiveness in Heaven above.
His arms everlasting, drove out the enemy,
defeating death and hell, He secured my eternity.

Thank you Lord for saving my soul.

1 Peter 2:24 "He himself bore our sins" in his body on the cross, so that we might die to sins and live for righteousness; "by his wounds you have been healed."

THE 3:16 FROM THE KINGS CROSS

Don't miss the last train home!
It's the 3:16 to Eternity,
A one way ticket to the throne,
All-inclusive by the Crystal sea.

Don't miss the last train home,
It's the 3:16 to Eternity!
A one way ticket to the throne;
Direct access to the heavenly city.

Don't miss the last train home,
It's the 3:16 to Eternity!
A one way ticket to the throne,
A master class in carpentry.

Don't miss the last train home!
It's the 3:16 to Eternity!
A one way ticket to Eternity.
Free from sin that's a certainty.

Don't miss the last train home!
It's the 3:16 to Eternity,
A one way ticket to the throne,
Where love is the only currency.

Don't miss the last train home,
It's the 3:16 to Eternity!
A one way ticket to the throne!
An audience with the King is my plea.

Please don't miss the last train home;
The 3:16 from the King's cross is here!
The station's full but not everyone is going!
So climb aboard and have no fear!

Don't miss the last train home .....

John 3:16 For God so loved the world that he gave his one and only Son, that whoever believes in him shall not perish but have eternal life.

A sinners prayer:

God I admit that I'm a sinner. I believe that you sent Jesus, who died on the cross and rose from the dead paying the penalty for my sins. I am asking that you forgive me my sin and I receive your gift of eternal life. It is in Jesus name that I ask for this gift, Amen.

ABOUT THE AUTHOR
ALAN KEMP

I am a 46 year old man but an 8 years young child of God, with a tendency to stumble and fall (messing up is not an option, we're all sinners, it happens), and time and time again, God picks me up.

An Englishman rooted in little old Nor'n Ireland, married to Allison (an Ulster lass) for 24 years, now surely that's a miracle and proof that prayer works and God is faithful in any ones' book. Born again just under 9 years ago, after Allison prayed for almost 20 years for my salvation with total faith in God. We have three amazing children: Poppy 21, Amber 18, and Peter 16. My only regret is it took so long to see how blessed I am to have them.

Becoming a Christian, everyone will tell you, is the last thing they would have expected from me. I was real, the world was real and God was not. The irony of it all is my first conversation with Allison was a hard hearted debate on the existence of God and how troubled Northern Ireland should simply be abandoned as a lost cause, how ironic. God really does have a sense of purpose and a sense of humor.

So to the writing, where did this all come from? It was never my intention, my hobby, my passion, or plan to write. My heart was always hard, cold, and closed BUT GOD poured his love in and released me from the demons that kept me silent, allowing the emotions that I and no one else thought existed to be expressed.

Many of my poems are written without awareness of the words, until the pen stops moving and then, tears! Others evolve as the Lord takes me on a journey, teaching me His Word in a very unique way. Many times I have sat in Church or at a meeting and before its even began, I have summarized the message to come in a poem, which, let me tell you, is quite a shock, but beautiful too.

So what started out as a few scribbles became the outpouring of emotion and truth that the Lord formed into Poetry. A friend encouraged me to post a few online and in a few short years, I have connected with many people worldwide and my Poetry has reflected the journey my life has taken and the passion the Lord has fueled in me.

Some people write to tell their story, express their thoughts or reach the unreachable. Some people of the world write because they long to live forever. I simply write because I want others to live forever.